THE

TRADING BLUEPRINT

Beginner's Ultimate
Guide to Mastering
the Markets...

|INTRODUCTION|

"Welcome to a world where opportunity meets strategy, where every trade holds the potential for growth. As you embark on this journey, discover the power of informed decisions, the art of risk management, and the thrill of unlocking financial potential. This book is your guide to navigating the intricate landscape of trading, empowering you to make confident choices and chart your course towards success."

| CONTENTS |

Alexander Elder

"The goal of a successful trader is to make the best trades. Money is secondary."

Victor sperandeo

" The key to trading success is emotional discipline. If intelligence were the key, there would be a lot more people making money trading."

Chapter One:

INTRODUCTION TO TRADING

- ## Understanding the Basics: What is Trading?

Trading, at its essence, is akin to a bustling marketplace where individuals and entities engage in the buying and selling of various financial instruments, ranging from stocks and currencies to commodities and derivatives.

Let's break it down: Imagine you're an art enthusiast who stumbles upon a limited-edition painting at a local auction. You purchase it, foreseeing its potential value surge due to the artist's rising popularity. Later, as predicted, the artist gains international acclaim, and the painting's value skyrockets, allowing you to sell it for a substantial profit. This scenario mirrors the fundamentals of trading—buying an asset, anticipating its appreciation, and then selling it at a higher price.

In real-world financial markets, this happens every day. Consider the stock market: investors acquire shares of a company at a certain price, speculating that its value will increase.

For instance, when Apple launched the iPhone, its stock value surged as the product's success translated into increased profits for the company, thereby raising the stock's worth. Investors who had earlier bought Apple shares reaped significant profits by selling them at the heightened price.

This example illustrates the essence of trading—predicting market movements and capitalizing on them to generate profits.

Trading isn't confined to stocks alone; it extends to other financial instruments. Take the foreign exchange (forex) market, where currencies are bought and sold.

For instance, imagine a traveler planning a trip to Europe when the euro is weaker against the dollar. Sensing that the euro might strengthen in the future, the traveler exchanges their dollars for euros. Later, when the euro indeed appreciates in value against the dollar, the traveler exchanges the euros back into dollars, profiting from the strengthened euro.

These real-life examples showcase the essence of trading—anticipating market trends, seizing opportune moments, and making informed decisions to maximize gains. Understanding these basics is the cornerstone for those venturing into the dynamic realm of financial markets.

• The Evolution of Trading: From Past to Present

Trading has a long history that's kind of like watching technology evolve. Back in ancient times, people swapped goods they had too much of for things they needed more. It's like trading your extra veggies for someone else's tools—a fair deal that helped everyone. As time moved on, markets started growing in cities, becoming busy places for trade. Just like today, people gathered to buy and sell things, but back then, it was more about bartering goods rather than using money.

Fast forward to the medieval times when traders traveled along famous routes like the Silk Road, connecting the East and the West. Picture caravans of camels carrying spices, silk, and other treasures. People didn't just trade goods; they exchanged ideas, cultures, and knowledge. These trade routes helped civilizations thrive and learn from each other.

Then came a game-changer: stock markets. It's like buying a piece of a company rather than a thing. Imagine you love gaming and believe a gaming company is going to be huge. You buy a part of that company, hoping its success will boost the value of your share. When it does, you can sell it for more money. That's the stock market, and it's been around for a few hundred years now.

Nowadays, with the internet, trading happens in the blink of an eye. You can buy or sell stocks, currencies, and more with just a few clicks. It's as easy as ordering your favorite food online. Everything happens super fast, and people from all over the world can trade without being in the same place.

For example, think about cryptocurrencies like Bitcoin. People buy them online, thinking their value will rise. When it does, they sell it to make a profit. Bitcoin started as a digital idea and became a big deal, even though it's not like regular money.

Trading has come a long way from swapping goods to buying pieces of companies and even digital currencies. Today's trading, with its lightning-fast pace and global reach, is a testament to how far this age-old practice has journeyed into the modern world.

- **Importance of Trading in Today's World:**

Trading stands as a cornerstone in today's global economy, playing a pivotal role not only in individual wealth generation but also in the growth and sustenance of large corporations and entire economies. At its core, trading isn't solely confined to the realm of the rich; it's a mechanism through which wealth is cultivated and industries flourish.

Prominent figures like Warren Buffett and Elon Musk exemplify how trading propels wealth creation. Buffett's strategic investments in companies with long-term potential, holding onto them until they appreciate significantly, and Musk's adept maneuvering in futuristic industries, illustrate how trading serves as a tool for individuals to grow their fortunes.

Trading holds immense significance in the global economy, where its effects ripple across sectors and nations. For instance, consider the New York Stock Exchange (NYSE), where billions of dollars' worth of stocks are traded every day. In 2021 alone, the total market capitalization of NYSE-listed companies surpassed $30 trillion, reflecting the sheer scale of trading's influence on the economy.

This activity isn't just about making money; it drives economic growth. When companies succeed and their stock prices rise due to trading activities, they attract more investors. This influx of capital empowers companies to expand, innovate, and hire more employees. It's like a cycle: successful trading fuels company growth, which, in turn, fuels economic development.

Beyond individual wealth, trading is intricately tied to the success of large corporations. Consider technology titans such as Apple, Google (Alphabet Inc.), and Amazon.

These companies, through their presence in the stock market, offer shares of ownership to the public, inviting investment in their growth and prosperity. The influx of investments via trading becomes the lifeblood that nurtures their expansion and innovation.

For instance, Amazon's strategic use of funds raised through trading has powered its expansion into diverse sectors. The company's ability to build new warehouses, innovate with services like Amazon Prime, and venture into cloud computing has been fueled, in part, by the capital amassed through trading activities.

The significance of trading in the economy extends far beyond individual companies. It influences sectors as diverse as technology, retail, finance, and healthcare, fostering growth and development on a grand scale. Consider the tech behemoth Apple Inc. Its success in the stock market reflects its innovative products and global appeal. In 2021, Apple's market capitalization soared beyond $2 trillion, making it one of the most valuable companies globally. This success isn't just about the company; it's about the industries it influences. The Apple ecosystem drives economic activity in areas like app development, manufacturing, and retail. For instance, the App Store ecosystem facilitated over $643 billion in billings and sales in 2020, benefiting millions of app developers worldwide. This illustrates how a company's success through trading stimulates industries, creating jobs and economic opportunities.

Trading isn't only about established giants; it also fosters startups and emerging businesses.

Take the case of Tesla, led by Elon Musk. In 2020, Tesla's market cap soared above $600 billion, surpassing industry stalwarts like Toyota and Volkswagen. Tesla's growth, largely influenced by trading activities, has stimulated the electric vehicle industry, prompting traditional automakers to invest heavily in electric car technologies. Moreover, venture capitalists utilize trading to fund startups. In 2021, venture capital funding in the U.S. surpassed $150 billion, helping new businesses grow, innovate, and contribute to economic dynamism.

Trading isn't merely a tool for the wealthy to grow their fortunes; it's a foundational element that drives economic growth, innovation, and progress. The impact of trading spans from individual investors making informed decisions to the collective influence on the growth trajectories of multinational corporations and emerging startups.

Chapter Two:

GETTING STARTED WITH TRADING

• Setting Clear Goals and Expectations:

When you're just starting with trading, it's like setting off on a journey—you need to know where you're headed. Imagine planning a road trip. Before hitting the road, you'd decide your destination, plan the route, and set milestones along the way. Similarly, in trading, having clear goals and expectations is crucial. It's not just about making money; it's about knowing what you want to achieve and how you'll get there.

For example, let's say you're interested in buying stocks. You might set a goal to save a certain amount of money to invest and decide how much risk you're willing to take. Maybe your goal is to grow your investment by a certain percentage over a year. That's your destination—the end goal you're working towards.

Having realistic expectations is key. It's like understanding that a road trip might have detours or delays. In trading, it's essential to know that not every trade will be a win.

Take it from experienced traders like George Soros or Paul Tudor Jones. They've seen their fair share of ups and downs. Soros, known for his big bets, experienced losses too. In 1992, when he made a successful bet against the British pound, he also faced losses along the way. Similarly, Jones, another successful trader, knows that not every trade will go as planned. Understanding this helps manage expectations and emotions when things don't go as expected.

Additionally, having a clear plan is crucial. It's like having a GPS guiding you on your road trip. A trading plan outlines your strategies, risk tolerance, and when to enter or exit trades.

Let's take a simple example: imagine you're buying a stock. Your plan might involve doing research, setting a budget, deciding when to buy, and most importantly, knowing when to sell if things don't go as planned. This plan acts as a roadmap, keeping you focused and helping avoid impulsive decisions.

It's important to review and adjust your goals and plans as you go. Just like recalculating your route if there's a road closure on your trip, in trading, you might need to adjust your strategies based on market changes.

Let's say your goal was to make a 10% return on your investment, but the market conditions change, and it becomes unrealistic. Adapting your goals to market realities is essential to stay on track.

Setting clear and realistic goals, managing expectations, having a solid plan, and adapting to changes are crucial steps when starting with trading. Just like a well-planned road trip, having a clear direction and being flexible along the way can lead to success in the trading journey.

- **Choosing the Right Market: Stocks, Forex, Commodities, Cryptocurrencies:**

Trading is like deciding which road to take on a journey—you need to choose the path that suits you best. There are various markets to explore: stocks, forex (foreign exchange), commodities, and cryptocurrencies. Each market has its characteristics, risks, and potential rewards, much like different roads offering diverse experiences.

Stocks are like shares of a company—you buy a piece of a business. For instance, companies like Apple, Microsoft, or Amazon offer stocks. In 2021,

Amazon's stock price soared above $3,000 per share, while Apple's market capitalization surpassed $2 trillion, reflecting their value in the stock market.

Investing in stocks means becoming a part-owner of these companies, sharing in their successes and losses. Stocks can be a great option for long-term investments, but they also involve risks linked to company performance and market fluctuations.

Forex, or the foreign exchange market, is like trading currencies. It's about exchanging one currency for another, such as trading U.S. dollars for euros. For instance, in 2021, the euro-to-dollar exchange rate fluctuated between $1.17 and $1.23, showcasing the currency's volatility. Forex trading offers opportunities to profit from changes in currency values, but it involves Understanding global economies, geopolitical events, and interest rate fluctuations.

Commodities include tangible goods like gold, oil, or agricultural products. Take gold, for example. Its price often fluctuates due to factors like economic instability or inflation. In 2021, the price of gold per ounce ranged from around $1,700 to $1,900, showing its volatility as a commodity. Investing in commodities allows diversification in a portfolio and can act as a hedge against inflation or economic uncertainties.

Cryptocurrencies are digital currencies like Bitcoin or Ethereum. These have gained popularity, with Bitcoin reaching an all-time high of nearly $65,000 in 2021. Cryptocurrencies operate on blockchain technology and are known for their volatility. They offer potential high returns but also come with significant risks due to their speculative nature and regulatory uncertainties.

Choosing the right market depends on factors like your risk tolerance, investment goals, and understanding of market dynamics. For instance, if you prefer stability, stocks of established companies might suit you. If you're comfortable with risk and volatility, cryptocurrencies might be intriguing. The key is to research, understand the market you're entering, and start with small investments to gain experience before diving in deeper. Just like picking the right road for a journey, choosing the right market in trading sets the direction for your investment journey.

- **Understanding Risk and Reward:**

Trading is like a journey filled with turns, and understanding the risks and rewards is like knowing which roads might have potholes and which ones might offer scenic views. When you start trading, you're venturing into a world where risks and rewards go hand in hand. Let's break it down:

The Risk: Trading involves the possibility of losing money. Just like in life, there's no guarantee that every trade will turn a profit. For instance, imagine investing $1,000 in a stock. If the stock price drops, you might end up losing part or all of your investment. Take GameStop's stock frenzy in early 2021. Some people saw its price skyrocket, investing in hopes of quick profits. However, when the price plummeted, many faced significant losses. This illustrates how sudden market changes can lead to unexpected losses.

The Reward: On the flip side, successful trades can bring in profits. Picture this: you invest in a company's stock at $50 per share, and later, the price rises to $100 per share. Selling it at this higher price means doubling your investment. Similarly, consider the meteoric rise of cryptocurrencies like Dogecoin. In 2021, Dogecoin, which started as a joke, saw its value soar, making early investors substantial profits. These examples show the potential for gains in trading.

How it Works: Trading involves weighing these risks against potential rewards. It's about making informed decisions and managing risks. For instance, diversifying investments—spreading money across different assets— can help reduce risks. Imagine investing in various stocks rather than putting everything into one. If one stock drops, the others might balance it out. Moreover, setting stop-loss orders—predefined limits on how much you're willing to lose on a trade—can help mitigate losses.

Understanding market trends, conducting research, and staying updated with news and events impacting markets are essential. For example, during the COVID-19 pandemic, industries like travel and hospitality took a hit due to lockdowns, impacting related stocks. Being aware of such events helps anticipate market movements and make informed decisions.

Additionally, it's crucial to manage emotions. Emotions can lead to impulsive decisions that might not align with your trading plan. Just like staying calm during unexpected roadblocks on a trip, maintaining a level head in trading is vital to making rational choices.

Chapter Three:

UNDERSTANDING FINANCIAL MARKETS

- **Exploring Different Financial Markets:**

Financial markets are like a big shopping mall with various sections offering different products. Each section, whether stocks, bonds, forex, or derivatives, has its unique offerings and attractions. Let's take a stroll through these markets:

Stock Market: Think of the stock market as a marketplace where companies sell ownership stakes. It's like owning a piece of a business. Stocks offer potential growth and dividends when companies perform well. Investors often look to invest in companies they believe will grow over time, aiming to profit from rising stock prices or regular dividend payments.

Bond Market: Bonds are like loans—you lend money to governments or companies, and in return, they pay you back with interest. For instance, the U.S. Treasury bonds offered an interest rate of around 1.5% in 2021.

Bonds are considered more stable than stocks and can act as a reliable source of income for investors seeking steady returns.

Forex (Foreign Exchange) Market: Forex trading involves the exchange of currencies, capitalizing on their price fluctuations. Investors speculate on currency pairs, aiming to profit from changes in exchange rates. Forex is known for its liquidity and the ability to trade 24/7 due to its global nature. Forex trading involves profiting from currency fluctuations by buying low and selling high.

Derivatives Market: Derivatives are financial contracts whose value depends on an underlying asset, like stocks, commodities, or interest rates. Options and futures contracts are common examples. They give you the right to buy or sell an asset at a specified price. Imagine it as reserving a product at a set price before deciding whether to buy it. Derivatives offer flexibility in managing risk or speculating on price movements without owning the underlying asset. In 2021, the options market in the U.S. saw trading volumes surpassing 7 billion contracts.

Commodities Market: This market deals with tangible goods like gold, oil, or agricultural products. Investors trade commodity futures contracts, aiming to profit from price changes. Commodities provide diversification and can act as a hedge against inflation or market uncertainties.

Among these markets, the stock market often attracts significant investor attention due to its potential for long-term growth. It's a popular choice for those seeking higher returns, although it also comes with higher risks. Bonds, on the other hand, are favored by risk-averse investors looking for stability and predictable income streams. Forex appeals to traders looking for liquidity and around-the-clock trading opportunities, while derivatives offer tools for managing risk and potential gains. Commodities, with their tangible nature, serve as an alternative investment and a hedge against economic uncertainties.

Understanding how these markets work involves recognizing their unique features, risks, and rewards. Stocks offer ownership, bonds provide steady income, forex deals with currencies, derivatives offer flexibility, and commodities hedge against inflation. Exploring these markets is like browsing through different shops at the mall—each has something distinct to offer.

• Market Participants: Who's Who in Trading?

In the world of trading, there are diverse participants, each playing a unique role, much like different characters in a story.

First off, we have individual traders, like you and me. These traders operate in the markets with their personal funds, buying and selling assets. Think of them as adventurers exploring the markets to make profits. Some traders, like George Soros, made substantial profits through bold bets. In 1992, Soros bet against the British pound, earning around $1 billion when the pound's value dropped significantly. Individual traders vary in strategies and risk appetites, some seeking short-term gains while others focusing on long-term investments.

Next, we have institutional investors, the heavyweight players in the trading world. These include mutual funds, pension funds, and hedge funds. They manage large pools of money from various investors, making substantial investments in the markets. Warren Buffett, the legendary investor and CEO of Berkshire Hathaway, is an example. Buffett's investment strategy involves picking undervalued stocks and holding onto them for the long term. His investments in companies like Coca-Cola and American Express showcase his patience and belief in fundamental value.

Furthermore, investment banks play a crucial role. They facilitate trades for clients, provide financial advisory services, and engage in trading on their behalf. These banks, like Goldman Sachs or JPMorgan Chase, have dedicated teams working on market analysis, research, and trading strategies.

For instance, Goldman Sachs often advises large companies on mergers and acquisitions, influencing market dynamics.

Another essential participant is market makers. These are firms or individuals who provide liquidity by buying and selling securities to maintain market efficiency. They ensure there's always someone willing to buy or sell an asset, enhancing market liquidity. Citadel Securities, for instance, is a major market maker in the U.S., facilitating trades in various financial instruments.

Central banks are key players too. They regulate monetary policies and manage currency reserves. Take the Federal Reserve in the United States. It influences interest rates, impacting borrowing costs and economic growth. Central banks play a crucial role in stabilizing economies and ensuring financial stability.

Lastly, regulators oversee and regulate financial markets, ensuring fair practices and investor protection.

The Securities and Exchange Commission (SEC) in the U.S. is one such regulatory body, monitoring markets and enforcing rules to maintain market integrity.

Understanding these market participants is like knowing the characters in a play—each with its role shaping the storyline.

Individual traders seek profits, institutional investors move markets with their massive investments, investment banks facilitate transactions, market makers ensure liquidity, central banks manage monetary policies, and regulators safeguard fairness. Together, they form the intricate ecosystem of financial markets, influencing their dynamics and functioning.

• Market Trends and Influences:

Market trends and influences are like the winds that sway the direction of financial markets, shaping their movements and behaviors. These trends arise from a multitude of factors, much like how different ingredients create unique flavors in a recipe.

One of the earliest market influences dates back to the Dutch Golden Age in the 17th century when the tulip mania swept the Netherlands. During this time, the prices of tulip bulbs skyrocketed to extraordinary levels, reaching exorbitant values. For instance, a single tulip bulb could cost as much as a luxurious house.

This euphoria eventually led to a market crash, causing significant financial losses. This historical event illustrates how market trends, fueled by speculation and excessive optimism, can lead to irrational valuations and subsequent market collapses.

Moving ahead, let's consider how economic indicators shape market trends. Think of these indicators as signposts guiding market movements. For example, Gross Domestic Product (GDP), which measures a country's economic output, significantly influences market sentiment. When GDP growth is robust, investors often feel optimistic about the economy's health, driving stock prices higher. Conversely, during economic downturns or recessions, like the 2008 financial crisis, when the U.S. housing market collapsed, stock prices plunged due to fears of economic instability.

Moreover, geopolitical events act as powerful market influencers. These events, much like unexpected storms, can shake financial markets.

Take the oil crisis in the 1970s. Political tensions in the Middle East led to an oil embargo, causing oil prices to skyrocket. This upheaval affected global economies, leading to inflation and economic turmoil worldwide. Similarly, more recent events like Brexit, the United Kingdom's decision to exit the European Union, created uncertainty, causing fluctuations in stock markets and currency values.

Another crucial influence is technological advancements. Imagine technological innovations as engines driving market evolution. The dot-com bubble of the late 1990s saw an unprecedented surge in internet-related stocks, with companies like Amazon and Cisco reaching astronomical valuations.

However, when many of these companies failed to deliver profits, the bubble burst, leading to significant market downturns. This showcases how technological trends can create market euphoria but also lead to subsequent corrections.

Understanding market trends and influences involves recognizing the impact of historical events, economic indicators, geopolitical tensions, and technological advancements on financial markets. It's like deciphering the forces that steer a ship in various directions. By grasping these influences, investors gain insights into market movements, enabling them to navigate turbulent waters and make informed investment decisions.

Chapter Four:

FUNDAMENTAL ANALYSIS

• Basics of Fundamental Analysis:

Fundamental analysis is like peeling layers of an onion to understand the core value of a company. It's a method used to evaluate the intrinsic value of stocks by examining factors that influence a company's true worth. Think of it as investigating the ingredients of a recipe to understand its taste and quality. This analysis primarily focuses on two key aspects: qualitative and quantitative factors.

Qualitative factors include evaluating a company's management, competitive advantage, and brand strength. For example, consider Apple Inc. Its strong brand and innovative products have led to a loyal customer base, contributing to its success.

On the other hand, quantitative factors involve analyzing numerical data, such as financial statements, earnings reports, and key ratios. These figures paint a picture of a company's financial health. For instance, examining a company's profit margins, revenue growth, and debt levels helps assess its financial stability. For example, a high debt-to-equity ratio might indicate a company's higher reliance on borrowed funds, which could pose risks.

There are various methods used in fundamental analysis, much like different tools in a toolbox.

One common approach is the discounted cash flow (DCF) method. This method estimates a company's value by forecasting its future cash flows and discounting them back to their present value. It's like predicting future income and adjusting it for today's value.

Another method is the Price-to-Earnings (P/E) ratio, which compares a company's stock price to its earnings per share. Investors use this ratio to gauge whether a stock is undervalued or overvalued compared to its peers.

Fundamental analysts also consider macroeconomic factors like interest rates, inflation, and government policies. These external factors impact a company's operations and its industry as a whole. For example, changes in interest rates can affect borrowing costs for companies, influencing their profitability.

Additionally, industry-specific factors, such as technological advancements or regulatory changes, also play a vital role in fundamental analysis. Consider the impact of regulatory changes on the healthcare industry, affecting pharmaceutical companies' earnings and stock prices.

Fundamental analysis involves a meticulous examination of both qualitative and quantitative factors to gauge a company's true value. It's like scrutinizing various puzzle pieces to see the complete picture. By delving into a company's financial health, competitive position, and industry dynamics, fundamental analysis helps investors make informed decisions about buying or selling stocks based on a company's real worth.

- **Economic Indicators and their Impact:**
  Economic indicators are like gauges on a dashboard, providing crucial insights into the health of an economy. They help investors understand how an economy is performing, much like checking vital signs to gauge someone's health.

  These indicators come in various forms, such as Gross Domestic Product (GDP), unemployment rates, consumer price index (CPI), and retail sales. They give us clues about an economy's strength, stability, and growth potential.

  One of the fundamental indicators is Gross Domestic Product (GDP), which measures the total value of goods and services produced within a country's borders. Think of it as a scoreboard showing the country's economic performance. For instance, during the Great Depression in the 1930s, the U.S. experienced a significant GDP contraction, indicating economic distress. Similarly, in the 2008 financial crisis, the U.S. GDP declined, signaling an economic downturn.

Unemployment rates are another critical indicator. They measure the percentage of people actively seeking employment but unable to find jobs. High unemployment rates, such as those witnessed during the Great Recession, indicate economic challenges, while low rates signify a robust job market. For example, in the early 2000s, the dot-com bubble burst led to job losses in the technology sector, impacting the overall unemployment rate.

Moreover, the Consumer Price Index (CPI) measures the average change in prices consumers pay for goods and services. It's like tracking how the cost of groceries or fuel changes over time.

During times of high inflation, like in the 1970s when oil prices surged, the CPI rose significantly, affecting consumers' purchasing power. Conversely, during periods of deflation, prices might fall, impacting businesses' revenues.

Retail sales, representing consumer spending, also act as indicators. They reflect consumer confidence and economic health. For instance, during economic downturns, consumer spending often declines as people tighten their budgets. However, during economic upswings, increased spending indicates a healthy economy. In the early 2000s, after the 9/11 crisis, retail sales plummeted due to reduced consumer confidence and fears of economic instability.

Understanding these economic indicators involves recognizing their impact on investors, businesses, and policymakers. They serve as guideposts for investors to make informed decisions, businesses to strategize operations, and governments to formulate policies. By monitoring these indicators, investors can anticipate market movements, businesses can adjust their strategies, and policymakers can implement measures to stabilize economies during economic fluctuations.

- **Company Analysis and Financial Statements:**
  Company analysis involves dissecting a company's financial health, much like a doctor examines a patient's vital signs. This analysis primarily revolves around financial statements, which are like report cards showcasing a company's performance. There are three main financial statements: the income statement, balance sheet, and cash flow statement.

Firstly, the income statement, also known as the profit and loss statement, highlights a company's revenues, expenses, and profits over a specific period. It's like a scoreboard showing a team's performance during a game. For example, if a company's revenue exceeds its expenses, it records a profit. Conversely, if expenses surpass revenue, it incurs a loss. The income statement provides insights into a company's ability to generate profits.

Secondly, the balance sheet resembles a snapshot of a company's financial position at a specific point in time, showcasing its assets, liabilities, and shareholders' equity. Imagine it as a snapshot of someone's savings, debts, and net worth. For instance, if a company's assets exceed its liabilities, it has a positive net worth. On the contrary, if liabilities outweigh assets, it indicates potential financial risks.

Lastly, the cash flow statement tracks the inflow and outflow of cash within a company, reflecting its liquidity and cash management. It's like tracking your personal income and expenses. For example, if a company generates more cash from its operations than it spends on investments, it signifies healthy cash flow. Conversely, negative cash flow might indicate liquidity issues.

Analyzing these statements involves assessing various financial ratios derived from the numbers within them. One key ratio is the debt-to-equity ratio, which measures a company's leverage by comparing its debt to its shareholders' equity. A high debt-to-equity ratio might signal higher financial risk, while a lower ratio indicates less reliance on borrowed funds. Another essential ratio is the return on equity (ROE), which measures a company's profitability relative to its shareholders' equity. Higher ROE signifies efficient use of shareholders' funds.

Analyzing a company's financial statements involves examining its historical data and comparing it to industry benchmarks and competitors. This comparison helps gauge a company's performance relative to its peers. Additionally, looking at trends over time reveals a company's growth trajectory and potential future performance.

Understanding company analysis and financial statements involves interpreting these reports to evaluate a company's profitability, financial stability, and growth prospects. Just as a doctor diagnoses a patient's health through vital signs, analyzing financial statements helps investors assess a company's financial well-being before making investment decisions.

Chapter Five:

TECHNICAL ANALYSIS

• Introduction to Technical Analysis:

Technical analysis is like reading the patterns in the stars to predict the weather—it's a method used to forecast future price movements of stocks or financial instruments based on past market data, primarily focusing on price and volume.

Think of it as deciphering clues from historical charts to anticipate future market trends. It relies on the belief that historical price movements repeat themselves and can help predict future market directions.

One of the key components of technical analysis is charting. Charts are like maps showing the price movements of stocks or assets over time.

The most common type of chart is the candlestick chart, displaying the opening, closing, high, and low prices for a specific period. For instance, observing a series of ascending candlesticks might indicate an upward trend, while a series of descending ones might suggest a downward trend.

Technical analysts use various tools and indicators to identify patterns and trends in market data. Moving averages, for example, smooth out price fluctuations over a specific period, helping analysts identify trends. A crossover between short-term and long-term moving averages might signal a change in trend direction. Another popular tool is the Relative Strength Index (RSI), which measures the magnitude of recent price changes to determine overbought or oversold conditions in a market.

Additionally, support and resistance levels are essential concepts in technical analysis. Support is like a floor preventing prices from falling further, while resistance acts as a ceiling preventing prices from rising higher. When prices approach these levels, they might bounce back or break through, indicating potential changes in market direction. For instance, if a stock repeatedly fails to rise above a certain price level (resistance), it might indicate a barrier to further price increases.

Understanding technical analysis involves recognizing patterns and trends in price charts and applying various indicators and tools to anticipate future price movements. It's like spotting shapes in clouds to predict weather changes. By studying historical price data and identifying repeating patterns, technical analysts aim to predict future price movements, enabling traders and investors to make informed decisions about buying or selling assets.

However, it's important to note that while technical analysis can provide valuable insights into market trends, it's not foolproof and doesn't guarantee accurate predictions. Market dynamics can be influenced by various factors beyond historical data, such as news events, economic indicators, or unexpected developments. Therefore, technical analysis is often used in conjunction with other forms of analysis to form a comprehensive view of the market.

- **Chart Patterns and Trends:**

Chart patterns and trends are like footprints left behind by the market, offering insights into potential future price movements. These patterns help analysts identify recurring formations in price charts, aiding in predicting potential market directions.

There are various types of chart patterns, each with its characteristics and implications.

Head and Shoulders: This pattern resembles a head between two shoulders and indicates a potential trend reversal. The head represents a peak, while the shoulders are two lower peaks. When the price breaks below the "neckline" connecting the lows of the two shoulders, it might signal a trend change from bullish to bearish or vice versa.

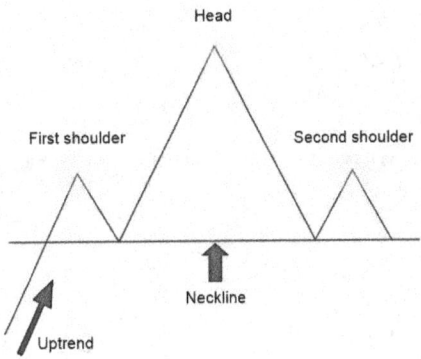

Double Top and Double Bottom: A double top pattern forms when a stock reaches a high price twice and fails to break through, indicating a potential trend reversal. Conversely, a double bottom pattern occurs when a stock hits a low price twice and fails to go lower, suggesting a potential upward reversal.

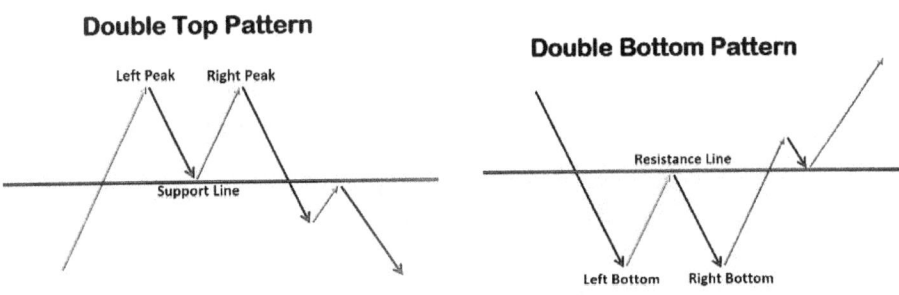

Flags and Pennants: These patterns represent short-term consolidations or pauses in a trend. Flags resemble rectangles, while pennants look like small symmetrical triangles. After a strong price movement (flagpole), the flag or pennant formation suggests a brief pause before the continuation of the previous trend.

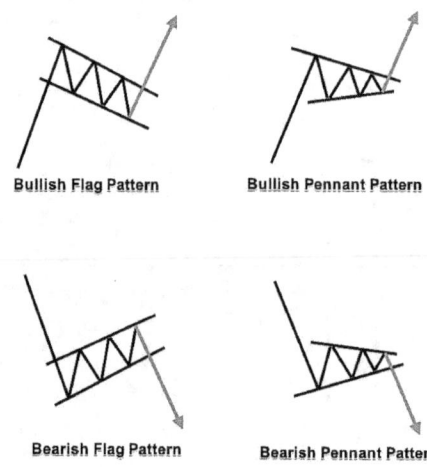

Bullish Flag Pattern · Bullish Pennant Pattern

Bearish Flag Pattern · Bearish Pennant Pattern

Cup and Handle: This pattern appears as a rounded bottom (cup) followed by a small consolidation (handle). It indicates a potential bullish continuation, with the handle representing a temporary consolidation before further upward movement.

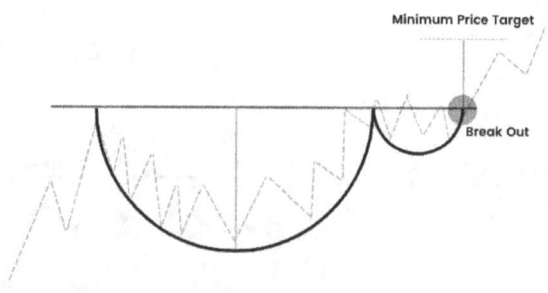

Minimum Price Target

Break Out

Triangles: Triangles come in various forms—ascending, descending, and symmetrical. Ascending triangles show a flat top and rising bottom, while descending triangles have a flat bottom and descending top. Symmetrical triangles have converging trendlines. These patterns indicate a potential breakout, with the price likely moving in the direction of the breakout.

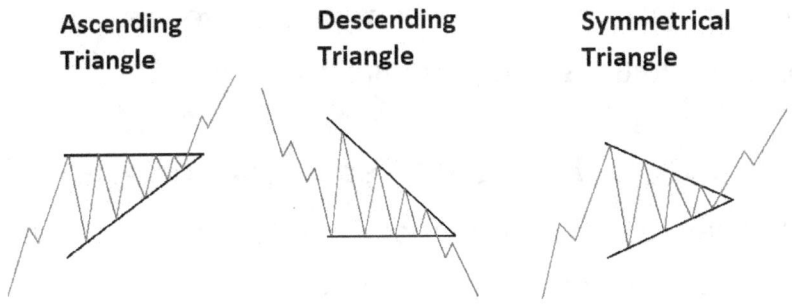

| Ascending Triangle | Descending Triangle | Symmetrical Triangle |

Recognizing these patterns involves understanding their formations and implications. For instance, when spotting a head and shoulders pattern after a prolonged uptrend, it might signal a potential trend reversal to the downside. Conversely, identifying a cup and handle pattern in a stock's chart might indicate a continuation of an upward trend.

Analyzing trends is crucial in technical analysis. Trends can be classified as uptrends, downtrends, or sideways trends. An uptrend consists of higher highs and higher lows, indicating a bullish market sentiment. Conversely, a downtrend comprises lower highs and lower lows, signaling a bearish market sentiment. Sideways trends, also known as consolidation, show price movements within a defined range, lacking a clear direction.

Understanding these patterns and trends aids analysts in making informed predictions about potential market movements. However, it's essential to combine chart patterns and trends with other technical indicators and fundamental analysis for a comprehensive view of market conditions and potential outcomes.

- **Indicators and Tools for Technical Analysis**:
  Indicators and tools in technical analysis are like the magnifying glasses and measuring tapes used by detectives—they help investors uncover clues and measure market dynamics. These tools assist in interpreting price movements and identifying potential trends or reversals.
  There are various categories of indicators and tools used by analysts to analyze market data.

  Moving Averages: Moving averages smooth out price data by creating a single flowing line on a chart, helping analysts identify trends. For instance, a simple moving average calculates the average price of a stock over a specified period. A crossover of short-term and long-term moving averages might signal a change in trend direction.

Relative Strength Index (RSI): RSI measures the magnitude of recent price changes to determine overbought or oversold conditions in a market. It ranges from 0 to 100, with values above 70 indicating overbought conditions and values below 30 indicating oversold conditions. Traders often use RSI to identify potential reversal points.

MACD (Moving Average Convergence Divergence): MACD combines two moving averages to generate trading signals. It consists of a MACD line and a signal line. When the MACD line crosses above the signal line, it might signal a bullish trend, while a cross below the signal line might indicate a bearish trend.

Bollinger Bands: Bollinger Bands consist of a middle band (simple moving average) and two outer bands representing standard deviations from the moving average. They indicate volatility and potential price reversals. When prices touch the upper band, it might suggest an overbought condition, while touching the lower band might signal an oversold condition.

Fibonacci Retracement: This tool helps identify potential support and resistance levels based on the Fibonacci sequence. Analysts use these levels to anticipate potential price movements. For instance, after a significant price movement, retracements to specific Fibonacci levels might indicate potential areas of price reversals.

Using these indicators and tools involves understanding their functions and applying them effectively. For instance, traders might use moving averages to confirm trends or identify potential entry or exit points. RSI helps assess whether a stock is overbought or oversold, aiding in decision-making. MACD provides signals for potential trend changes or momentum shifts.

Analysts often combine multiple indicators to validate their findings and reduce the risk of false signals. However, it's important to note that no single indicator or tool guarantees accurate predictions. Market dynamics are influenced by various factors, and using multiple tools helps in making more informed decisions but doesn't eliminate risks entirely.

By applying these indicators and tools effectively, investors can gain insights into market trends, potential reversals, and entry or exit points for trading or investment decisions. It's like assembling pieces of a puzzle to form a clearer picture of market conditions, enabling informed actions in the dynamic world of finance.

Chapter Six:

DEVELOPING A TRADING STRATEGY

• **Creating Your Trading Plan:**

Creating a trading plan is like charting a roadmap before embarking on a journey—it's a crucial step for traders to define their strategies, goals, and risk management techniques. A trading plan outlines a trader's approach to the market, covering aspects such as trade objectives, entry and exit criteria, risk tolerance, and money management strategies.

1. Define Your Goals: Begin by setting clear and achievable goals. For instance, a goal could be to achieve a specific percentage of return on your investment within a certain timeframe. Having a well-defined goal helps in creating a structured plan.

2. Choose Your Trading Style: Determine your preferred trading style based on your personality, time availability, and risk tolerance. Are you inclined towards day trading, where positions are opened and closed

within a day, or swing trading, where positions are held for several days to weeks? Understanding your style helps in selecting suitable strategies.

3. Set Entry and Exit Rules: Define specific criteria for entering and exiting trades. For example, a trader might decide to enter a trade when the price breaks above a certain moving average or exits when the price reaches a predetermined profit target or hits a stop-loss level.

4. Manage Your Risks: Implement risk management strategies to protect your capital. Decide on the maximum amount or percentage of your account you're willing to risk on a single trade. For instance, you might decide not to risk more than 2% of your account on any single trade to minimize potential losses.

5. Maintain Discipline: Stick to your plan and avoid emotional decision-making. Discipline is crucial in trading. Even if a trade doesn't go as planned, following your pre-defined rules helps maintain consistency and control over your trading activities.

Let's consider an example: Sarah, a beginner trader, decides to create her trading plan. She sets her goal to achieve a 10% return on her investment within six months. Sarah chooses swing trading as her preferred style due to her part-time availability. Her entry rule is to buy a stock when its price crosses above the 50-day moving average, and her exit rule is to sell when the price hits a 15% profit target or a 5% stop-loss level. Sarah decides to risk no more than 2% of her account balance on any single trade to manage risks effectively.

Here's a simple representation of Sarah's trading plan:

- Goal: Achieve a 10% return within six months.
- Trading Style: Swing Trading (holding positions for several days to weeks).
- Entry Rule: Buy when price crosses above the 50-day moving average.
- Exit Rule: Sell when price hits a 15% profit target or a 5% stop-loss level.
- Risk Management: Risk no more than 2% of account balance on any single trade.

By crafting a clear and concise trading plan, beginners like Sarah can maintain focus, manage risks effectively, and stay disciplined in their trading activities, increasing the likelihood of achieving their trading goals.

- **Risk Management: Protecting Your Capital**

Risk management in trading is like safeguarding your savings in a storm—it's a set of strategies and techniques designed to protect your capital from potential losses while engaging in market activities. It involves assessing and mitigating risks associated with trading to ensure the preservation of your investment. Effective risk management allows traders to control the amount they're willing to lose on any single trade, minimizing the impact of losses on their overall account.

1. Determine Risk Tolerance: Understand your risk tolerance—the level of risk you're comfortable taking. This depends on factors like your financial situation, investment goals, and emotional resilience. Beginners often have lower risk tolerance levels, preferring to minimize potential losses.

2. Use Stop-Loss Orders: Implementing stop-loss orders is a fundamental risk management tool. A stop-loss order is like an insurance policy—it automatically closes a trade at a predetermined price to limit losses. For instance, if a trader buys a stock at $50 and sets a stop-loss at $45, the trade will automatically close if the price drops to $45, limiting the loss to $5 per share.

3. Position Sizing: Determine the size of your positions relative to your account size and risk tolerance. Beginners often allocate a small portion of their account, typically around 1-2%, to each trade. For example, with a $10,000 account and a 1% risk per trade, the maximum risk per trade would be $100.

4. Diversification: Spread your investments across different assets or sectors to reduce the impact of potential losses on your overall portfolio. Diversification helps in mitigating the risks associated with a single asset's performance.

5. Risk-Reward Ratio: Evaluate the potential rewards against the risks before entering a trade. A favorable risk-reward ratio ensures that potential profits outweigh potential losses. For example, a trader might aim for a risk-reward ratio of 1:2, meaning they risk $100 to potentially make $200 on a trade.

Let's consider an example: John, a beginner trader, decides to manage his risks effectively. He assesses his risk tolerance and determines it's 2% of his $5,000 trading account. John buys stock ABC at $50 per share and sets a stop-loss at $45, defining his maximum loss per share at $5. With a 2% risk tolerance, John calculates that he can buy 20 shares of stock ABC ($100 maximum risk per trade / $5 maximum loss per share = 20 shares).

Here's a simple representation of John's risk management plan:

- Risk Tolerance: 2% of $5,000 account ($100 per trade).
- Stop-Loss Order: Set at $45 per share for stock ABC.
- Position Size: Buy 20 shares of stock ABC ($100

maximum risk / $5 maximum loss per share).
• Risk-Reward Ratio: Aim for a 1:2 ratio to ensure potential profits outweigh potential losses.

By following these risk management strategies, beginners like John can protect their capital, minimize potential losses, and create a disciplined approach to trading, fostering long-term success in the dynamic world of financial markets.

• **Backtesting and Refining Strategies:**

Backtesting is like practicing a sport before a big game—it's a process used by traders to evaluate their trading strategies using historical market data. It involves applying a strategy to past market conditions to assess its effectiveness and performance. This allows traders to analyze how a strategy would have performed in the past, providing insights into its potential success in current market conditions.

1. Gathering Historical Data: Begin by collecting historical market data relevant to the asset or market you intend to trade. This data typically includes price movements, volumes, and other relevant indicators for the chosen time frame.

2. Defining the Trading Strategy: Develop a clear and specific trading strategy with entry and exit rules. For

instance, a strategy might involve buying a stock when its price crosses above a moving average and selling when it crosses below another moving average.

3. Applying the Strategy: Apply the defined strategy to historical market data. Manually or using specialized software, simulate trading decisions based on the strategy's rules using past market conditions.

4. Assessing Performance: Analyze the results of the backtest to evaluate the strategy's performance. This includes calculating metrics such as the percentage of winning trades, maximum drawdown (largest peak-to-trough decline), and overall profitability.

5. Refining the Strategy: Based on the backtest results, refine and adjust the strategy as needed. This might involve tweaking entry or exit criteria, altering risk management techniques, or optimizing parameters to improve performance.

Let's consider an example: Sarah, a beginner trader, develops a simple moving average crossover strategy. She uses historical data for stock XYZ over the past year. Her strategy involves buying the stock when the 50-day moving average crosses above the 200-day moving average and selling when the opposite occurs. She backtests this strategy using historical data and finds that it resulted in 70% winning trades and a maximum drawdown of 5%.

Here's a simple representation of Sarah's backtesting process:

- Trading Strategy: Buy stock XYZ when the 50-day moving average crosses above the 200-day moving average and sell when it crosses below.
- Backtesting Period: Historical data for stock XYZ over the past year.
- Performance Metrics: 70% winning trades and a maximum drawdown of 5%.

Upon analyzing the results, Sarah notices that while the strategy generated a high percentage of winning trades, the drawdown was relatively low. She refines her strategy by adjusting the moving average parameters and risk management techniques to further optimize its performance.

By backtesting and refining trading strategies, beginners like Sarah can gain insights into the historical performance of their strategies, identify potential strengths and weaknesses, and fine-tune their approaches to increase the likelihood of success in live trading scenarios.

Chapter Seven:

BROKERS AND TRADING PLATFORMS

• **Choosing the Right Broker:**

Brokers are intermediaries or financial institutions that facilitate trading activities in various financial markets, connecting traders or investors to the market. They act as the bridge between individuals and the financial markets, allowing clients to buy or sell assets such as stocks, bonds, commodities, currencies, or derivatives.

There are different types of brokers, including:

1. Full-Service Brokers: These brokers offer a wide range of services beyond just executing trades. They provide investment advice, research reports, retirement planning, and more. However, their services often come with higher fees.

2. Discount Brokers: These brokers offer fewer services but execute trades at lower costs. They usually provide online platforms for clients to conduct their own

research and make trading decisions independently.

3. Online Brokers: With the advent of the internet, online brokers provide trading platforms accessible through the internet, allowing clients to trade from anywhere with an internet connection. They offer varying levels of service and fees.

Selecting the right broker is akin to picking the right tool for a job—it's a crucial decision for traders as brokers act as intermediaries facilitating access to financial markets. Here are key factors to consider when choosing a broker:

Regulation and Security: Begin by ensuring the broker is regulated by a reputable financial authority. Regulatory bodies oversee brokers' operations, ensuring they comply with industry standards and safeguard clients' funds. For instance, in the United States, brokers regulated by the Securities and Exchange Commission (SEC) or the Commodities Futures Trading Commission (CFTC) are considered trustworthy.

Trading Fees and Commissions: Evaluate the broker's fee structure, including commissions, spreads, and other charges. Different brokers have varying fee models— some charge commissions per trade, while others offer commission-free trades but might have wider spreads.

For example, Broker A charges $5 per trade, while Broker B offers commission-free trades but has a slightly wider spread.

Trading Platforms and Tools: Assess the trading platforms and tools offered by the broker. A user-friendly and efficient trading platform is essential for executing trades smoothly. Look for features like real-time market data, charting tools, and order types available. For instance, Broker A provides a robust and easy-to-navigate platform, while Broker B offers more advanced tools but with a steeper learning curve.

Asset Selection: Consider the variety of assets available for trading. Whether you're interested in stocks, forex, commodities, or cryptocurrencies, ensure the broker offers a diverse range of tradable assets that align with your investment preferences. Broker A might specialize in stocks, while Broker B provides a broader range of assets, including cryptocurrencies.

Customer Support: Evaluate the broker's customer service and support. Accessibility to responsive customer support, especially during trading hours, is crucial in case of any issues or queries. Test their customer service through different channels like phone, email, or live chat to gauge their responsiveness and helpfulness.

Account Minimums and Leverage: Consider the minimum account balance required to open an account with the broker. Additionally, if you plan to utilize leverage, understand the broker's leverage offerings. Some brokers offer higher leverage, which can amplify both gains and losses.

Let's consider an example: John, a beginner trader, is looking for a suitable broker. He assesses two brokers—Broker A and Broker B. Broker A is regulated by a reputable authority, charges $5 per trade, offers a user-friendly platform, and specializes in stocks. On the other hand, Broker B is also regulated, offers commission-free trades but with wider spreads, provides an advanced trading platform, and offers a broader range of assets, including cryptocurrencies.

After comparing the features, John decides that Broker A aligns better with his preferences as a beginner trader focusing on stocks and prioritizing a user-friendly platform over a broader asset selection.

By considering these factors and comparing different brokers, beginners like John can make informed decisions when choosing a broker that best suits their trading needs and preferences, setting a solid foundation for their trading journey.

• Understanding Trading Platforms:

A trading platform is like a command center for traders—it's a software interface provided by brokers that allows individuals to access financial markets and execute trades. These platforms come in various forms, from basic web-based interfaces to advanced software with comprehensive tools and features.

Here's how they work and what traders need to know:

Access to Markets: Trading platforms provide access to various financial markets, including stocks, forex, commodities, cryptocurrencies, and more. They allow traders to view real-time market data, such as prices, charts, and order book information.

Order Execution: Traders can place different types of orders using these platforms, such as market orders (buy or sell at the current market price), limit orders (buy or sell at a specified price), and stop-loss orders (automatically sell a security when it reaches a certain price to limit losses).

Charting and Analysis Tools: Trading platforms offer charting tools and technical indicators to help traders analyze market trends, patterns, and potential entry or exit points. These tools include moving averages, RSI,

MACD, and various chart types like candlestick and line charts.

Customization: Many trading platforms allow customization based on traders' preferences. They might offer the ability to create watchlists, set up personalized alerts, and arrange layouts to suit individual trading styles.

Mobile Accessibility: Most modern trading platforms offer mobile applications, enabling traders to access markets and execute trades from smartphones or tablets, providing flexibility and convenience.

For example, let's consider Sarah, a beginner trader. She uses a trading platform provided by her broker to trade stocks. The platform displays real-time stock prices, charts showing historical price movements, and a variety of order types. Sarah can place a market order to buy or sell a stock at the current price or set a limit order to buy or sell at a specific price.

Sarah also utilizes the charting tools available on the platform, like moving averages and candlestick charts, to analyze stock price movements. She sets up personalized watchlists to monitor her favorite stocks and receives alerts when certain price levels are reached.

Trading platforms serve as essential tools for traders, providing access to markets, order execution capabilities, analysis tools, and customization options. They empower traders to make informed decisions, execute trades efficiently, and manage their investment portfolios effectively in the dynamic world of financial markets.

- **Account Types and Trading Costs:**

   1. Account Types: Brokers offer various types of accounts to suit different trading needs and preferences:

   - Cash Account: This is a basic trading account where traders use their cash to buy stocks or other assets. With a cash account, traders can only trade using the funds available in the account.

   - Margin Account: A margin account allows traders to borrow money from the broker to trade, increasing their buying power. This enables traders to potentially amplify gains or losses. However, it's crucial to understand the risks associated with using leverage in margin accounts.

   - Retirement Accounts: These accounts, such as Individual Retirement Accounts (IRAs) or 401(k)s, offer tax advantages for retirement savings. They may have specific limitations on the types of trades or contributions allowed.

2. Trading Costs: Trading involves various costs that traders need to consider:

• Commission Fees: Brokers may charge fees for executing trades, usually referred to as commission fees. These fees can vary based on the broker, account type, and the size of the trade. For instance, a broker might charge $5 per trade or a percentage of the trade value.

• Spread: In addition to commission fees, some brokers charge a spread—a difference between the bid (selling) and ask (buying) price of an asset. Wider spreads may increase trading costs.

• Other Fees: Brokers might levy additional fees for services like account maintenance, inactivity, wire transfers, or data subscriptions. It's essential to understand these fees before opening an account.

For example, John is considering opening a trading account. He evaluates different account types offered by brokers. He opts for a margin account to potentially increase his trading flexibility. However, he's aware of the risks associated with borrowing funds. John also compares commission fees across brokers and finds one charging $5 per trade, which suits his trading frequency and budget.

When John starts trading, he places a buy order for 100 shares of a stock. He incurs a $5 commission fee for this trade. Additionally, if the broker charges a spread of $0.05 per share, he needs to account for an extra $5 as part of the trading cost due to the spread ($0.05 spread per share * 100 shares = $5).

Understanding different account types and trading costs helps traders make informed decisions based on their trading objectives, risk tolerance, and budgetary considerations. By selecting the right account type and being aware of associated costs, beginners like John can manage their trading activities more effectively.

Chapter Eight:

EXECUTING TRADES

- **Understanding Execution and Order Types:**

1. Market Order: A market order is like ordering food at a restaurant—you're willing to buy or sell at the current market price, aiming for immediate execution. When placing a market order, you're prioritizing speed over price. For example, if you want to buy shares of a company immediately, you place a market order specifying the number of shares, and the broker executes the trade at the best available price in the market.

2. Limit Order: A limit order is more like setting a specific budget for a purchase—you specify the price at which you're willing to buy or sell an asset. For instance, if a stock is currently trading at $50 per share but you're only willing to buy it if the price drops to $45, you can place a limit order at $45. The trade will only execute if the stock's price reaches or goes below $45.

3. Stop Orders: Stop orders are similar to triggers—they become active once the market reaches a specified price. There are two types of stop orders:

• Stop-Loss Orders: These orders are used to limit potential losses. For instance, if you bought a stock at $60 and want to sell it if the price drops to $55 to prevent further losses, you place a stop-loss order at $55.

• Stop-Buy Orders: These orders are used to enter a position when the market reaches a specific price. For example, if a stock is trading at $70, but you believe it's a good buy if it reaches $75, you can place a stop-buy order at $75. If the stock's price hits $75 or higher, your order will execute, initiating a buy.

4. Trailing Stop Orders: This type of order moves in tandem with the asset's price. It's beneficial for locking in profits while allowing room for the asset to grow. For instance, if a stock is trading at $100 and you set a trailing stop order at $95 with a trailing amount of $5, the stop price will move up as the stock's price rises. If the stock's price falls by $5 from its peak value, the order will execute, helping secure profits.

For example: John wants to buy shares of Company X but only if the stock price drops to $45 or less. He places a limit order at $45. If the stock's price falls to $45 or below, John's order will execute at $45 or the best available price at that time.

Let's consider another example: Sarah wants to buy shares of Company X. She's ready to pay the current market price, so she places a market order for 100 shares. The broker immediately executes the trade at the best available price in the market, which might be slightly different from the displayed price due to market fluctuations.

Next, Sarah wants to purchase shares of Company Y, but she believes the stock is overpriced at the moment. She places a limit order at $55 per share, lower than the current market price of $60. The trade will only execute if the stock's price drops to $55 or below.

Additionally, to manage her risks, Sarah purchases shares of Company Z at $70 per share and sets a stop-loss order at $63. If the stock's price declines to $63 or lower, the stop-loss order triggers, automatically selling her shares to limit potential losses.

Understanding these different order types gives traders like John and Sarah the flexibility to control their trades according to specific prices, minimize potential losses, lock in profits, and enter or exit positions based on their predetermined criteria in the financial markets.

- **Managing Trades and Positions:**

  Monitoring Positions: Once you've opened a trade, it's essential to monitor its progress. Keep an eye on the asset's price movements, as they directly impact your trade's profitability. For instance, if you bought shares of Company A at $50 per share, you'll track the stock's price movements to assess whether it's rising or falling.

  Setting Stop-Loss and Take-Profit Orders: To manage risk and lock in profits, traders often set stop-loss and take-profit orders. A stop-loss order triggers an automatic sell if the asset's price reaches a predetermined level, limiting potential losses. Conversely, a take-profit order triggers a sell at a specified price to secure profits. For instance, if you bought shares at $50, you might set a stop-loss at $45 to limit losses and a take-profit at $60 to lock in profits.

  Adjusting Positions: Sometimes, market conditions change, requiring adjustments to your positions. This might involve trailing stop orders or modifying your stop-loss and take-profit levels based on new developments or technical analysis.

  Scaling In and Out: Traders also practice scaling in or out of positions. Scaling in involves gradually entering a position by buying or selling smaller amounts initially.

Scaling out involves gradually exiting a position by selling parts of it as the trade moves in the desired direction. For example, if you want to invest $10,000 in a stock, you might buy $2,000 worth first and add more as the stock moves favorably.

Risk Management: It's crucial to assess and manage risks associated with open positions. This involves calculating position sizes relative to your account size and risk tolerance. Traders often limit the amount of capital they risk per trade to a certain percentage of their account balance.

For instance, let's consider John, who bought shares of Company B at $100 per share. He sets a stop-loss order at $90 to minimize potential losses if the stock's price falls. Additionally, he sets a take-profit order at $120 to secure profits if the stock rises. As the stock's price climbs to $110, John decides to adjust his stop-loss order to $100 to protect some profits in case the price reverses.

Effectively managing trades and positions involves continuous monitoring, strategic use of stop-loss and take-profit orders, adjusting positions based on market conditions, and employing risk management techniques to optimize trading outcomes.

Chapter Nine:

PSYCHOLOGY OF TRADING

- **Mastering Emotional Intelligence in Trading:**

  Understanding Emotional Intelligence: Emotional intelligence refers to the ability to recognize, understand, and manage emotions effectively, especially in high-stress situations like trading. In trading, emotions often run high due to the potential for financial gains or losses. Emotional intelligence helps traders make rational decisions despite these emotional fluctuations.

  Controlling Emotions: One of the key aspects of emotional intelligence in trading is controlling emotions like fear, greed, and anxiety. Fear can lead traders to exit trades prematurely, while greed might prompt them to stay in a trade longer than they should. Anxiety can cause overtrading or impulsive decision-making.

  Developing Discipline: Emotional intelligence fosters discipline in trading. Discipline involves sticking to a trading plan, following predefined strategies, and not letting emotions sway decisions. For instance, if a trader has set a stop-loss at a certain level, discipline ensures they adhere to it, even if emotions urge them otherwise.

Practicing Mindfulness: Being mindful—being aware of one's thoughts, emotions, and reactions—can significantly impact trading decisions. Mindfulness allows traders to observe their emotions without being controlled by them. It helps in making more rational and less impulsive decisions.

Handling Losses: Emotional intelligence helps traders cope with losses. Losses are part of trading, but how traders react to them determines their success. Emotional intelligence helps in accepting losses as a natural part of the process, learning from them, and moving forward without being emotionally overwhelmed.

Mastering emotional intelligence in trading is an ongoing process that involves self-awareness, self-regulation, and effective decision-making despite emotional fluctuations. Traders who prioritize emotional intelligence can maintain a more balanced approach to trading, make better decisions, and ultimately improve their overall performance in the financial markets.

- **Dealing with Greed, Fear, and FOMO:**

    Greed often tempts traders to aim for overly ambitious profits or hold onto winning trades for too long. To counter this, it's essential to set realistic profit goals and adhere to them. Creating a trading plan with predefined profit targets helps maintain a disciplined approach, preventing the lure of unrealistic gains.

    Fear is a common emotion when facing potential losses. It can lead traders to exit trades prematurely, missing out on potential gains. Employing risk management tools like stop-loss orders helps limit potential losses while allowing trades to unfold without being solely influenced by fear.

    FOMO (Fear of Missing Out) arises when traders see others profiting from a trade and fear missing the opportunity. This emotion can lead to impulsive decisions without thorough analysis. Overcoming FOMO involves sticking to your own trading plan and strategies, avoiding chasing trends blindly based on others' successes.

    Effectively managing these emotions requires self-awareness and discipline. Recognizing when these emotions arise and having strategies in place to manage them can significantly enhance a trader's decision-making process, leading to more consistent and rational trading outcomes in the dynamic world of financial markets.

- **Building Discipline and Patience:**

    Trading discipline involves adhering to your trading plan rigorously. It means sticking to predefined rules, strategies, and risk management protocols regardless of emotions or external market influences. For instance, if your plan dictates a maximum risk of 2% of your capital on any single trade, maintaining that discipline helps preserve your capital in the long run, even in volatile markets.

    Patience in trading is about waiting for the right opportunities that align with your strategy. It involves refraining from impulsive actions and staying calm even during periods of market uncertainty. For instance, if a trader prefers trading specific chart patterns, exercising patience means waiting for those patterns to appear rather than forcing trades based on anticipation.

    Developing discipline and patience takes time and practice. It involves creating a well-defined trading plan, setting realistic goals, and following through consistently. Traders need to recognize that losses and missed opportunities are part of the process and should not sway them from their predefined strategies.

In essence, building discipline and patience is about following a structured approach, having a clear trading plan, and sticking to it. It's about controlling impulses, managing emotions, and maintaining consistency in decision-making. Traders who master discipline and patience often achieve more stable and successful outcomes in the dynamic realm of financial markets.

Chapter Ten:

ADVANCED TRADING STRATEGIES

- **Day Trading vs. Swing Trading vs. Long-Term Investing:**

   1. Day Trading: Day trading involves buying and selling financial assets within a single trading day to capitalize on short-term price movements. Traders executing day trades focus on quick entries and exits, often making numerous trades throughout the day. For instance, a day trader might buy 100 shares of a stock at $50 and sell them an hour later at $52, aiming to profit from the $2 per share increase.

   2. Swing Trading: Swing trading involves holding positions for several days or weeks to capture "swings" in the market. Swing traders analyze technical indicators and chart patterns to identify potential short-to-medium-term trends. For example, a swing trader might notice an upward trend in a stock's price, buy 200 shares at $60, and sell them a week later at $70, capitalizing on the $10 per share increase.

3. Long-Term Investing: Long-term investing entails holding assets for extended periods, often years or decades, to benefit from long-term appreciation. Investors focusing on the long term conduct thorough fundamental analysis, considering factors like company growth and economic conditions. For instance, an investor might buy 500 shares of a company at $100 per share and hold them for several years as the stock appreciates to $300 per share, realizing a substantial gain over time.

Each strategy requires a unique skill set, risk tolerance, and time commitment. Day trading demands quick decision-making, intense focus, and the ability to manage risks within short timeframes. Swing trading requires patience, the ability to ride short-to-medium-term trends, and managing positions through market fluctuations. Long-term investing necessitates patience, a long-term view, and the ability to withstand market volatility without frequent trading.

Selecting the appropriate strategy hinges on individual preferences, risk tolerance, and financial objectives. Traders and investors need to align their trading styles with their strengths and goals to navigate the intricate landscape of financial markets successfully.

- **Options, Futures, and Derivatives:**

Options provide the right, but not the obligation, to buy or sell an asset at a predetermined price within a specified timeframe. There are two types: call options, giving the right to buy an asset, and put options, granting the right to sell an asset. For example, consider a trader buying a call option for 100 shares of a company at a strike price of $50. If the stock price rises above $50 within the option's timeframe, the trader can exercise the option and buy the shares at $50, even if the market price is higher.

Futures contracts obligate traders to buy or sell an asset at a predetermined price on a specified date in the future. These contracts standardize the terms, including quantity, quality, and delivery date. For instance, a trader might enter into a futures contract to buy oil at $60 per barrel in six months. If the market price exceeds $60 at the contract's expiry, the trader benefits from the lower purchase price agreed upon in the futures contract.

Derivatives are financial contracts derived from an underlying asset's value. They derive their value from other financial instruments and can include options, futures, swaps, and more. Derivatives allow investors to hedge risks, speculate on price movements, or gain exposure to various assets. For example, a trader might use a derivative contract to hedge against potential losses in a stock portfolio by betting on a different asset's price movement.

These financial instruments offer unique opportunities for traders and investors but also carry risks. Options and futures involve leverage, meaning a small movement in the underlying asset's price can lead to substantial gains or losses. Derivatives, including options and futures, require a good understanding of market dynamics and may not be suitable for beginners due to their complexity.

For example, consider a trader using options to hedge against potential losses in a stock portfolio. By buying put options on an index that moves inversely to the portfolio's performance, the trader can potentially offset losses if the market declines.

- **Algorithmic and Quantitative Trading:**
Algorithmic and quantitative trading employ computer programs and mathematical models to make trading decisions in financial markets. Algorithmic trading involves using predefined instructions to automatically execute trades based on specific criteria. These algorithms analyze market data and execute trades without human intervention. Quantitative trading, on the other hand, relies on mathematical models and statistical

analysis to identify trading opportunities. It involves creating strategies based on historical data and complex calculations to predict market movements.

For instance, imagine a hedge fund using algorithmic trading. They've programmed an algorithm to buy a certain stock if its price drops by 3% within a minute. As soon as the stock hits that percentage decline, the algorithm swiftly executes the buy order, capitalizing on the predetermined criteria.

Quantitative trading, meanwhile, could involve a trader using statistical models to identify patterns in market data. This trader might develop a strategy based on historical price movements, identifying specific trends and using statistical methods to predict future price movements. They might then automatically execute trades based on these predictions.

These strategies aim to take advantage of market inefficiencies and patterns that might be difficult for humans to spot or act on quickly. However, implementing such strategies requires a solid understanding of programming, mathematics, and market dynamics. Additionally, there are risks involved, such as technological failures, sudden market changes, or errors in the algorithm's design.

As technology advances, these trading strategies continue to evolve, incorporating machine learning and artificial intelligence for more sophisticated analysis. Traders navigating these strategies need to stay informed about technological advancements and market changes to use these tools effectively in the ever-changing landscape of financial markets.

Chapter Eleven:

REVIEWING AND IMPROVING

• Tracking and Evaluating Performance:

Evaluating and tracking performance in trading is akin to navigating using a compass; it provides direction, helps avoid pitfalls, and enables continuous improvement. Let's delve deeper into this vital aspect:

Tracking Performance:

At the heart of successful trading lies meticulous record-keeping. Traders maintain detailed logs of their trades, documenting entry and exit points, trade duration, position size, profits or losses, and the rationale behind each trade. These records serve as a valuable repository of trading history, offering a comprehensive view of a trader's actions over time. For instance, a trader might meticulously note that out of 30 trades made in a month, 18 were profitable, indicating a 60% success rate.

Evaluating Performance:

The evaluation phase involves dissecting the tracked

data to unearth insights that drive improvements. Traders analyze their records to pinpoint strengths, weaknesses, patterns, and inefficiencies in their strategies. This critical analysis provides a clear picture of what's working and what needs refinement. For instance, a trader might realize through evaluation that their strategy consistently underperforms during volatile market conditions, prompting them to recalibrate their approach or implement risk management tools to mitigate losses during such times.

Key Metrics for Assessment:

Traders rely on various performance metrics to gauge success and refine their strategies. One such metric is the win-loss ratio, which measures the number of profitable trades against losing ones. A high win-loss ratio suggests more successful trades, while a lower ratio indicates room for strategy improvement. Additionally, traders consider the risk-to-reward ratio, assessing the potential profit against the risk taken in each trade. A favorable risk-to-reward ratio signifies that the potential profit outweighs the risk undertaken, enhancing the overall profitability of the trading strategy.

For example, a trader scrutinizing their performance may discover a win-loss ratio of 2:1, denoting that for every two winning trades, they have one losing trade. However, upon deeper analysis, they realize that the average profit from winning trades is significantly smaller than the average loss from losing trades. This insight prompts a reevaluation of their risk management strategy to ensure that gains offset losses more effectively.

Benefits of Tracking and Evaluating Performance:
The process of tracking and evaluating performance is akin to a compass guiding traders through the intricate maze of financial markets. It empowers traders to identify patterns, capitalize on strengths, address weaknesses, and make informed decisions. Regular review and analysis of trading performance facilitate adaptability to evolving market conditions, risk minimization, and the enhancement of overall profitability.

• Learning from Mistakes and Successes:

Learning from mistakes and successes is an invaluable aspect of trading that shapes traders' growth and future decisions.
In the world of trading, mistakes and successes go hand in hand. Mistakes are not failures but rather learning opportunities. They offer insights into what doesn't work and pave the way for improvement. On the other hand, successes are not just victories but valuable lessons too. They shed light on what strategies or decisions were effective and should be replicated.

Analyzing Mistakes:

When a trade goes awry, it's essential to dissect the reasons behind it. Was it impulsive decision-making? Poor risk management? Misinterpretation of market indicators? By reviewing the mistakes made, traders gain clarity on what led to the undesired outcome. For instance, a trader might analyze a losing trade and discover that they ignored a crucial technical indicator before entering the trade, leading to a substantial loss.

Leveraging Successes:

Similarly, when a trade turns out profitable, it's essential to understand why it succeeded. Was it thorough analysis? Effective risk management? Clear entry and exit points? Examining successful trades helps traders identify patterns and strategies that contributed to positive outcomes. For example, a trader might review a successful trade and recognize that it was the result of meticulous research and timing, leading to significant gains.

Implementing Lessons Learned:

The key to progress in trading lies in implementing lessons from both mistakes and successes. Traders often create journals or logs to record not only their trades but also the lessons learned from each experience. By doing so, traders avoid repeating the same mistakes and capitalize on successful strategies. For instance, a trader might learn from a mistake of overleveraging and adjust their risk management strategy to avoid similar pitfalls in the future.

Growth Through Continuous Learning:

Trading is an ongoing learning process. Embracing mistakes and successes as opportunities for growth fosters continuous improvement. Traders who actively seek to learn from their experiences, adapt their strategies, and remain open to new ideas are better positioned to navigate the dynamic and unpredictable nature of financial markets.

Trading isn't just about making profits; it's about learning and evolving. By analyzing mistakes and successes, traders acquire valuable insights, refine their strategies, and progressively enhance their trading prowess. Remember, in the world of trading, every mistake is a potential lesson, and every success is a testament to effective decision-making and strategy.

• Continuously Improving Your Trading Skills:

Continuously improving trading skills is akin to sharpening a tool in a toolkit; it enhances a trader's ability to navigate the complexities of financial markets. Let's explore this concept in simpler terms:

Embracing Lifelong Learning:

Trading is a journey of continuous learning. The ever-evolving nature of financial markets necessitates a commitment to ongoing education and skill enhancement. Traders need to stay abreast of market trends, economic indicators, and technological advancements impacting trading strategies. This commitment to learning equips traders with the tools to adapt and thrive in dynamic market conditions.

Seeking Education and Resources:

Traders often explore a multitude of resources to bolster their skills, ranging from books, online courses, webinars, and mentorship programs to gain insights and deepen their understanding of trading concepts. For instance, a trader might enroll in a technical analysis course to understand chart patterns better, thereby improving their ability to predict market movements.

Utilizing Simulations and Practice:

Practice is pivotal in honing trading skills. Many traders utilize simulations or demo accounts offered by brokerage platforms to practice strategies in a risk-free environment. These simulations mirror live market conditions, allowing traders to test new strategies, refine techniques, and build confidence without risking real capital.

Networking and Mentorship:

Engaging with fellow traders and seeking mentorship from seasoned professionals can accelerate skill development. Networking provides opportunities to exchange ideas, discuss strategies, and gain insights from diverse experiences. Mentorship programs enable beginners to learn from experienced traders, benefiting from their guidance and expertise.

Setting Goals and Reviewing Progress:

Setting specific, measurable goals helps traders focus on areas requiring improvement. For instance, a trader might set a goal to achieve a certain win-loss ratio or to refine a specific trading strategy within a set timeframe. Regularly reviewing progress against these goals allows traders to assess their development and adjust their approach accordingly.

The Path to Mastery:

Trading skills, like any other skill, require dedication, patience, and persistence. Consistent effort in seeking education, practicing strategies, and learning from both successes and failures propels traders towards mastery. Every setback is an opportunity to learn, adapt, and refine strategies for future success.

Chapter Twelve:

THE FUTURE OF TRADING

- **Emerging Trends and Technologies:**

The Digital Transformation:

    Trading is undergoing a digital metamorphosis, embracing technologies that promise efficiency, speed, and accessibility. One such trend is the rise of algorithmic trading, where computer algorithms execute trades at lightning speed based on predefined criteria. This technological leap not only enhances trade execution but also allows for intricate strategies that respond swiftly to market changes.

Blockchain and Cryptocurrencies:

    The advent of blockchain technology has given rise to cryptocurrencies, such as Bitcoin and Ethereum, transforming the landscape of financial transactions. Blockchain's decentralized and secure nature has sparked interest in the financial world. For example, decentralized finance (DeFi) platforms leverage blockchain to provide traditional financial services like lending and trading without intermediaries.

Artificial Intelligence (AI) and Machine Learning:

AI and machine learning are revolutionizing trading strategies. These technologies analyze vast amounts of data, identify patterns, and make predictions. Traders use AI to automate tasks, such as market analysis and trade execution. As an illustration, machine learning algorithms can analyze historical market data to identify trends and patterns, aiding traders in making more informed decisions.

Quantum Computing:

The future of trading may witness the integration of quantum computing, a cutting-edge technology with the potential to process vast amounts of data at unparalleled speeds. Quantum computers could revolutionize complex calculations and simulations, allowing traders to analyze market trends and risks with unprecedented efficiency. While quantum computing is still in its early stages, its potential impact on trading is a topic of anticipation and exploration.

Augmented and Virtual Reality:

Imagine a trader immersed in a virtual world, visualizing market trends and making decisions in a three-dimensional space. Augmented and virtual reality technologies offer a novel way for traders to interact with financial data. These immersive experiences could enhance data visualization and decision-making processes. While still in the experimental phase, these technologies hold promise for transforming the trading landscape.

Environmental, Social, and Governance (ESG) Investing:
    A notable trend shaping the future of trading is the emphasis on ESG factors. Investors are increasingly considering environmental, social, and governance criteria in their decision-making. Companies adhering to sustainable practices and ethical standards are gaining favor. This shift reflects a broader societal awareness and a growing demand for responsible and ethical investment practices.

The Power of Big Data:
    Big data analytics is becoming a cornerstone of effective trading strategies. Traders harness the power of big data to analyze market trends, sentiment, and economic indicators. This data-driven approach enables more accurate predictions and informed decision-making. For instance, analyzing social media sentiment can provide insights into market sentiment, influencing trading strategies.

• Adapting to Changing Market Conditions:

Navigating the ever-changing waters of financial markets demands a trader's ability to be agile and adaptable. Imagine markets as a living, breathing entity, influenced by various factors like economic shifts, global events, and unforeseen developments. Successful traders, much like skilled navigators, understand the importance of adjusting their strategies to ride the waves of market dynamics.

Adaptability in trading is not a one-size-fits-all concept but rather an art that involves flexibility in response to different market conditions. Picture a trader as a craftsman with a toolkit filled with diverse skills. When faced with heightened volatility, these traders are adept at fine-tuning their risk management strategies to navigate the stormy seas of unpredictable price fluctuations.

Balancing technical and fundamental analysis is akin to a delicate dance. Technical analysis involves studying historical price data and chart patterns, providing insights into trends. On the other hand, fundamental analysis delves into economic indicators and global events, offering a broader context for decision-making. Traders who seamlessly blend these analyses gain a comprehensive understanding of market conditions.

Risk management becomes a crucial aspect of this dance, where traders employ strategies like setting stop-loss orders and adjusting position sizes. It's a strategic move, like a tightrope walker adjusting their balance pole in response to unexpected challenges, ensuring stability in the face of potential risks.

Diversification is the trader's way of planting various crops to weather different financial climates. By spreading investments across diverse assets, industries, or regions, traders create a resilient portfolio that can withstand adverse conditions affecting specific sectors or asset classes.

Decoding economic indicators is like reading the signs in nature. Traders who are adept at adaptation closely monitor indicators such as GDP growth, unemployment rates, and inflation. Changes in these indicators act as early warnings, providing valuable insights into the economic climate and shifts in market sentiment.

Learning from market history is akin to understanding the footsteps of those who have walked the path before. Analyzing past market behaviors offers valuable lessons for crafting strategies in response to similar situations.

Remaining globally aware is essential for traders, just

as a keen observer of nature watches for changes in the environment. Staying informed about geopolitical shifts, policy adjustments, and major announcements allows traders to anticipate sudden shifts in market dynamics.

• Looking Ahead: Opportunities and Challenges

Peering into the future of trading is like forecasting the weather for financial markets. As we embark on this exploration, envision traders as meteorologists, equipped with tools to predict opportunities and challenges on the horizon.

Technological Innovations:

One significant aspect of the future lies in technological advancements. Imagine traders harnessing the power of artificial intelligence and machine learning, transforming data analysis into a more efficient and predictive process. These technologies can analyze vast datasets in real-time, helping traders make informed decisions swiftly. For instance, algorithmic trading, driven by complex algorithms, is gaining prominence, allowing for automated execution based on predefined criteria.

Digital Currencies and Blockchain:

Cryptocurrencies, like Bitcoin and Ethereum, are emerging players in the financial landscape. Picture them as the new currencies in this evolving ecosystem. Blockchain, the technology behind these digital currencies, ensures secure and transparent transactions. As cryptocurrencies gain wider acceptance, traders may find new avenues for investment and diversification.

Global Connectivity:

In the future, markets will be more interconnected than ever before. Think of it as a global village where information travels seamlessly across borders. Traders can access real-time data from various markets, allowing them to respond quickly to global events. This interconnectedness creates both challenges and opportunities, as fluctuations in one market may ripple across others.

Environmental, Social, and Governance (ESG) Investing:

Consider the rise of ESG investing as a growing trend. Traders are increasingly factoring in environmental, social, and governance considerations when making investment decisions. This shift reflects a broader awareness of the impact of businesses on the world. As sustainability becomes a focal point, traders may find opportunities in companies aligning with ESG principles.

Challenges in Market Regulation:

Looking ahead, anticipate the evolution of market regulations. Governments and regulatory bodies worldwide are likely to adapt to the changing landscape of trading. Striking a balance between fostering innovation and safeguarding market integrity will be an ongoing challenge. Traders need to stay abreast of regulatory changes to navigate the evolving regulatory landscape effectively.

Remote Trading and Flexible Work Arrangements:

Picture traders working from various corners of the world, connected virtually. The future of trading may witness an increase in remote trading facilitated by advanced technologies. This flexibility allows traders to adapt their work environments to suit their preferences, fostering a more diverse and inclusive trading community.

Cybersecurity Concerns:

As technology advances, so do the threats. Cybersecurity becomes a paramount concern in the future of trading. Traders must navigate a landscape where safeguarding sensitive information is as crucial as making profitable trades. Developing robust cybersecurity measures becomes imperative to protect against potential threats and attacks.

Quantifying Market Sentiment:

In the future, traders may have tools to quantify market sentiment with greater accuracy. Imagine sentiment analysis algorithms scouring news articles, social media, and other sources to gauge the mood of the market. Traders can then make more informed decisions by understanding the prevailing sentiment and potential market reactions.

www.ingramcontent.com/pod-product-compliance
Lightning Source LLC
Chambersburg PA
CBHW071157290526
45796CB00007B/66